The Super Simple Guide to CPS

By Lori Hamilton

Illustrated by Taylor Foust

ISBN: 1490950117
ISBN-13: 978-1490950112

DEDICATED

With gratitude to
Dawn, Sara, Kim and Shari

CONTENTS

LORI HAMILTON

There are entire government agencies devoted to protecting children against their own parents. According to the Department of Health and Human Services, there were 415,129 children in foster care as of September 30, 2014. Just less than half a million kids live with caregivers who are not their parents; however, the numbers are improving. In 2006 there were 510,000 children in the foster care system. In any case, the numbers are astounding.

The reasons for placement vary. Neglect, physical and sexual abuse, drug use and jail are some of the reasons children end up in the foster care system. In 2014, 46% lived in nonrelative foster homes, 29% lived in relative foster homes, 8 % were in institutions, 6% group homes, 5% were allowed home for trial visits in hopes of discharge from the foster care system, 4% lived with foster adopt families, 2% ran away, 1% lived independently under supervision, more than half had goals to return home.

More than a third of runaways had been in the foster care system at some point. A study done by Contra Costa County found that one third of foster children end up homeless and 35% get arrested while in the foster care system.

According to Childhelp.org, children who are sexually abused are 2.5 times more likely to abuse alcohol and 3.8 times more likely to develop some sort of drug addiction. Two thirds of people in treatment for drug abuse say they were abused as children. Children who are abused are 59% more likely to be arrested as a juvenile, 28% more likely to be arrested as an adult, and 30% more likely to commit a violent crime. Of these children, 30% will likely abuse their own kids and 80% of 21 years old adults who have been abused meet the criteria for at least one psychological disorder.

The annual cost of child abuse in 2012 was estimated at 80 billion dollars. These fees include hospitalization for serious injuries of mistreated children, mental health care for victims of abuse, child welfare services to protect neglected and abused children, law enforcement costs for interventions, special education, juvenile delinquency costs, mental and physical health care, and criminal justice costs for adults who were abused as children. The numbers are staggering and the statistics disheartening.

Part One

1

WHAT HAPPENED

Now that you have the system in your life, how do you get it

out? A good place to start is to look at what got you in trouble in the first place. Grab some paper and pen and begin to answer as many of the questions being asked as you can. What alerted the authorities? You might want to blame a neighbor for calling the cops, a teacher for filing a CPS report or maybe a therapist. Maybe the cops were jerks when they came. It really doesn't matter who called or who came, the issue is why they were called in the first place. What was the reason for the call? If possible look around. Try to look beyond the neighbor you hate, the teacher who has it out for you, the cop who made you feel like a loser. Don't waste time blaming. Blaming is a huge waste of time and energy. All the time wasted blaming others sounds like "blah, blah, blah" to a Social Worker and a Judge.

So what was the reason for the call? Did your child have a bruise? Did they wear dirty clothes? Was there a smell? Were you or another caregiver drunk or high? Did the neighbors hear screaming? Is there illegal activity in the home? The sooner you identify the issue within your home, the sooner you can move on. Is this the first time the cops have come to your house for some sort of problem or is it a regular occurrence? Do the cops know your family? Is your home a peaceful place or is there discord?

Only you know what is happening when no one is around. Are there family secrets? Is your life transparent? What would happen if someone dropped in unannounced?

Identify the problem, acknowledge the secret. Not all secrets need to be told, however anything that jeopardizes the stability of your child's home needs to be dealt with. This book is designed to help you navigate CPS and understand your responsibility to yourself and your child. Occasionally, someone is wrongly accused of mistreatment to a child, but not usually. Please do not resist what is now expected of you.

Many times parents are doing the best they know how. Generations of child abuse or neglect play an enormous role in a person's ability to care for their children. If your parents were unable to treat you with respect, then you might not have the ability to treat your own children with respect. Think back to your childhood. What do remember of your upbringing? Was there love and kindness? What did you like about your childhood and what did you hate? How do you want your children to remember their childhood, and do you care? If you really don't care, they might be better off in foster care. Your children will have memories of their childhood too, like you they will remember this experience

2

MANAGING MANDATES

First, take your list of mandates and look everything over, they are probably quite extensive. If your family has ended up in the system you will have a one-page list of mandates with your court paperwork, don't panic. If you've been down this road before, you may have to repeat classes you've already taken. Clearly, if you've been here before, a judge might assume you weren't paying attention the first time, or you don't care.

You will want a calendar and a planner. You will have numerous places to be; classes, visits, etc. and you will want to have every appointment on your calendar. You don't want to miss a thing, not one. Carry your planner everywhere and at the end of each day transfer all appointments to the calendar. Just this step in organizing your time will give you a sense of control. If you feel confused about when a class or appointment is scheduled, call immediately. Every night when you go to bed, you should know where you need to be the next day.

The other thing you might consider is an alarm clock, if your cell phone has one, great but make sure it's charged. A dead cell phone is not an acceptable excuse for anything. Many classes are in the early morning. This will be like a regular job so treat it with that sort of professionalism. There will be times when you feel overwhelmed and hopeless; unfortunately that's to be expected. Please, get up and put one foot in front of the other. Whining and complaining are a huge waste of energy at this point. You will need every ounce of emotional and physical energy to get through this period. In fact it is a perfect time to clean house. Literally clean house and clean up your life. Clean out anything that does not serve you and your kids for good. Anything that takes up unnecessary space. People, stuff, even pets can be a burden on an already struggling life.

This might also be a good time to enlist the help of your family. If you don't have a very good relationship with family, this might be a good time to make amends. It might not be possible. There are numerous reasons families can't make amends. There may be circumstances that prevent a relationship with family members. Call on people you have been able to count on in the past. Hopefully you haven't burned bridges to these important people.

I met a father from Mexico who had no family in the United States. He took his family to church every Sunday. A woman noticed this family and offered her support. She didn't know them, but she could see a need. He was slow to trust her, but with no one else to help out, he slowly got to know her. He was embarrassed by his life and felt like an outsider. Slowly he allowed her to get close, and there came a day when he needed support. She was there. She wasn't family, but was more like family than his own.

3

THE BALL AND CHAIN

You've read the statistics, now how will you remove this

enormous ball and chain? Check each mandate off your list.

Possible mandates might include parenting classes, therapy, drug

classes and testing, restitution, and supervised visits. Whatever the mandates, they will be your responsibility to take care of them. If you have a job, it will be tough. If you don't then you have plenty of time while your kids are away.

Managing mandates will be your full time job. There will be parenting classes, drug classes, therapy, and visits. Some of these things might be once a week, some twice. Make sure your schedule allows for all these things. Hopefully, you will be allowed two visits a week with your children, please don't miss any. If you're feeling exhausted and overwhelmed, you are probably meeting those mandates.

I can't say this enough, keep open communication with your social worker and foster parents. They can support you if you let them. It is the job of the social worker to keep your children safe. It may seem as if they are the enemy and you can feel any negative emotion you want; however, if your kids have been taken from you there is a reason. Now, that being said, most parents do the best they know how. It may not be good enough, but it's the best that they can do. It's time to learn how to parent. If you truly love your children, it would be wise to not only take your parenting classes but also participate. Read everything there is to read. Parenting doesn't come naturally to everyone. Some people don't bond with their kids easily. If you believe this is an issue that you struggle with, it doesn't mean you're a bad person but you might need to see a therapist to figure out why this is a problem.

Keep your list of mandates out where you can easily find them and read them every day. Review them daily and understand them. If you don't understand one or more, ask your social worker. You may not like the reason behind them, however you will need to follow these rules. Maybe you need to attend a drug class. Perhaps you don't feel you have a drug problem. Whether you do or don't isn't the issue, you will need to attend. Even if you haven't ever used anything more than caffeine. Show your cooperation and willingness to participate. Social workers need to see an understanding of what's happening. Again it is their job to protect your kids. The more you argue, the more they see a lack of understanding.

This story will give an example of a family who resisted for months before coming to an understanding. I met this family who had five kids and the kids were removed for neglect. The parents couldn't get the kids to their doctor appointments. One child who had a chronic illness and needed ongoing care. They had many excuses but no solutions. Their car was broken down or out of gas. The older kids had school. Dad was sick, mom was pregnant. This family was already in the reunification stage but still they couldn't pull it off. They frequently blamed the social worker for their problems. These people didn't have jobs, just excuses.

Finally, the kids were removed again. The kids were put in foster care, and given appropriate medical care. The parents visited irregularly, always having an excuse for not showing up. Finally, they showed up one day ready to work. Something clicked. Maybe it was the way the kids treated them at visits. Maybe all their supports got tired of trying to help people who wouldn't help themselves. The resistance was gone. When the parents stopped resisting so did everyone around them. The social worker returned calls, the kids were happy to see them and people offered support.

4

DRUG USE

If there are drugs being used or sold, that is a problem. Not only is it illegal, but it will definitely affect your child's placement. If it's not you, but your spouse or boyfriend/girlfriend, it's time to look at the relationship for what it is. If your significant other is using, abusing or selling drugs, there's a good chance they love drugs more than you. Consider drugs the other woman or man. It's usually a love affair with a very enchanting mistress. It is also possible this person doesn't care if the kids come back or not.

I met a dad whose kids were at risk for removal. This dad had no worries about his kids. He said "I was in foster care when I was a kid and I turned out alright." He felt he turned out alright, however he was on the verge of losing his kids. Did he turn out alright?

Now, if you are the parent using. Stop now and go to the nearest drug rehab. There are outpatient services available. They can help you decide if outpatient is enough or if you need inpatient care. Go. Just go. It doesn't matter if you don't believe there's a problem, just assume there is one. You will be tested regularly, and if there's even a trace of anything, it will be assumed you are abusing drugs. Truth is, you cannot care for others when you're high. If your kids were removed and there were drugs in the home, you will be required to go to drug class. Just take it upon yourself to go. Eventually you will be required to attend, but if you just do it before any mandate is given, the court will see your readiness to make things right. The good news is you will learn something about drug use, and when your kids come home, you will have something important to teach them.

Most parents want the best for their kids, and under the layers of drugs are usually good people. If you are willing to peel back the layers, you'll see the goodness come out; most importantly your kids will see it. Drugs tend to strip people of their emotions. Kids need caregivers with emotions, it's human nature. If you argue and fight with the system and insist there is no problem, it tends to make the situation worse. It shows you don't "get it." Of course the choice is always yours. If you take the needed steps your chances of regaining your kids and your life improves.

I once knew a mom who fought hard for her two small children, after being removed because of her drug use. Every time she slipped and used, she would stop fighting for her kids. When she was clean, she had the determination of a pit bull. Finally, after a couple of long years and nearly losing them for good, she got clean and that pit bull fight came back, so did her kids.

Turns out marijuana is legal in some states. I would urge that you not take this as a license to use, even if you have a license to use. If you have a medical marijuana license, please discuss it with your social worker. I would recommend full disclosure to your social worker. This will show that you are open and honest and willing to do whatever it takes. Remember, alcohol is legal and many people are forbidden from using, as a condition by the courts.

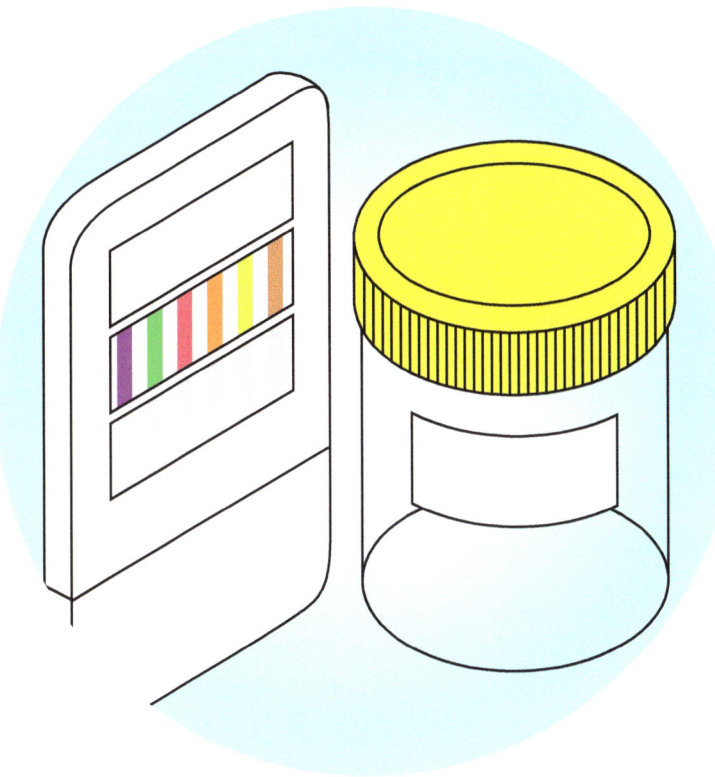

5

DRUG TESTING

The best liars and posers are drug users. They are also the worst liars and posers. Drug users will say they don't smoke dope while lighting a joint. Drug users will deny the pants they are wearing are theirs if there is a pipe in the pocket. They will avoid drug testing by saying they can't pee, and other interesting things.

They are the biggest excuse makers. Basically, if you're using, you may not be believed even when you're telling the truth.

Drug class are designed to teach you why drugs are bad. More than likely you know. People don't lie when the truth is good enough. I knew a family who smoked a lot of weed. They knew everything there was to know about marijuana. Not just how to grow and sell, but all the negative health and legal consequences with complete accuracy. I found them very educated on all aspects of marijuana, and when they weren't high, they were very open.

If you need a higher level of care, seek it out. You will be praised for your efforts. Not everyone can get a handle on addiction, but the harder you try, the better your chance for success and reunification.

As stated earlier in this book, some people can drink and others cannot. If you were mandated not to consume alcohol then stay away. Alcohol is a little harder as it is legal and most people have it readily available. This might be a good time to look at your friends and family and whom you choose to hang around. Decisions regarding good friendships and influences are not just for kids. Adults often have a hard time staying away from bad influences.

At some point all adults need to take a look at who they socialize with. You're not alone; it's a hard fact of life that some people are just not your friends.

Take note, if your friends have involvement with CPS, they probably aren't a good choice to hang out with.

6

ALCOHOL ABUSE

Alcohol is a tricky one. Some people drink and there are no issues, for some it's not possible. You may know people who drink beer every night after work or have a glass of wine and they have no one telling them that there is a problem. It's not a problem for everyone, but please consider this; it's legal, so for many people that means it's okay. Sometimes the mandates will state no drinking, but not always. If your friends and family have let you know that alcohol is a problem, that's good enough.

Again the resistance might be your problem, just follow the rules and don't resist them. Also, you might consider AA. If your family's wellbeing is affected by your attitude on alcohol, stop now.

Alcohol tends to make people emotional. The funny thing is, people usually turn to alcohol to take the edge off. For many it's relaxing in small doses. It's also a social thing to do. Hanging with friends, drinking can be a good time. Alcohol tends to bring out a person's emotions in surround sound. People cry, yell, fight and laugh to the extreme. Whatever is safely stuffed beneath the surface is now allowed to flow freely, like truth serum. When the cops show up at a domestic dispute, most of the time alcohol is involved.

I once knew a guy who was the life of the party when he started drinking and everybody loved to party with him early in the night. He bought drinks and said all the right things. It didn't take long before he was picking fights with innocent people, calling them names and going to jail. By the way, his kids hated him and his wife left him.

7

SHOW UP TO EVERY VISIT. EARLY.

The visits with your kids are a privilege. At the point which "the system" gets involved, you are now under a microscope. It would benefit you to be aware of your actions at all times. You now have no room for error and you will be expected to play by society's rules. A good place to start is with the visits. You will be expected to show up every time, on time.

Flu bug got you down? No money for gas? Flat tire? Buses running late? Earthquake? Tornado? Tsunami? There is no excuse for not attending a visit. No matter what the reason for your absence from the visit, it will be noted and remembered. Consequently, if you make them "when you can" those visits won't be noticed as much as the missed ones, just noted.

Arrive early. Always be 30 minutes early. It's best that you are the one waiting, not the children. Children don't like to wait, and it will be noticeable if they are unhappy because you were late. If there is any risk of traffic, plan for it. Again, no excuse will suffice. Be early. If by some act of God the road is closed and you will be late, use your cell phone and call the social worker and foster parent. If you don't have a cell phone, pull over and use a pay phone.

Bring a snack for the kids and their favorite toys. The visit is for them. Make it fun, so they feel relaxed. Remember they miss you terribly, so help them ease this difficult situation by bringing things they like. Make sure the snack is nutritious. Fruit, nuts, veggie sticks, crackers. When possible, stay away from sugary items, as the foster parents will have to pay the consequences of hyped up kids. This is also a good opportunity to practice your newly-learned parenting skills from your parenting class. The good news here is that you will have the opportunity to try things out and when the visit is over, you can assess how things went. If one skill didn't work, you can try another next time. If you're noticing the kids are struggling with your new parenting skills, don't worry it's new for them too. Keep working with your skills. Don't be afraid to ask your social worker their opinion on how you're doing, it shows you care.

A word about Foster parents. They are caring for your children. Treat them with the utmost respect. They may not parent the way you would like, but they are caring for the ones you love more than anyone. Don't speak poorly of them in front of your children. Also, ask the foster parents for updates. One family I knew, asked the foster mom to keep a baby book for her baby so she would know her baby's milestones. The foster mom happily did it and when the baby came home, she had a beautiful baby book complete with pictures. Foster families take their jobs seriously and most would love to do things for parents such as keep pictures and keepsakes.

Now those are just logical things you should do. There are many reasons to show up for visits and they aren't all just about looking good in the eyes of the Social Worker. There's also self-respect, the ability to get up in the morning and look yourself in the mirror and know you are doing everything within your ability to make things right.

You might also want to be able to live without guilt, that gut wrenching feeling you get when you know you're doing the wrong thing. Most of all your visits are for your kids. They miss you and need to know that you miss them too.

Hug them, kiss them, ask them how they are. Ask about school, their friends, the sports they play or like to watch. Compliment them and tell them they look beautiful. Tell them they are smart don't mention any flaws. The visits should be positive and upbeat. Give them reassurance of your love. They will probably ask if or when they can come home. Unfortunately you can't answer that question. Please don't burden them with court dates and lies. Unfortunately, court dates don't necessarily mean they are coming home, although sometimes they do, it's not a done

deal until the judge says it is. Don't even tell them they are

coming home. Some possible answers to that question are:

"I don't know, but I love you."

"I don't know, I miss you too."

"I don't know, but I can't wait to see you at the next visit"

The truth is you don't know. If you tell them they are coming

home and they don't, there will be more tension and anger.

8

ATTEND EVERY PARENTING CLASS

If you've been assigned to Parenting Classes, make sure you attend every one. Show up early, bring a notebook and pen, read the material, do the homework. Participate in every discussion and ask questions. Most of all listen and understand what is being taught. It is valuable information and you are there to learn.

It would appear to most Social Workers that you need to learn to be a parent. Parenting doesn't come naturally to everyone, therefore it would be wise to listen and ask questions. You won't be condemned for asking questions. If you have a good instructor, you will be encouraged to participate. Even parents who don't have involvement with "the system", benefit from some sort of parenting class.

Again, there are no excuses for not attending. If you are deathly ill, show up anyway and let the instructor decide if you are too sick to attend. Hopefully, you will be part of a lively group. Possibly, you can meet some others who will be of support to you.

The goal of any class you attend is to "get it". You should learn about acceptable and unacceptable discipline, problem solving and finding appropriate solutions to everyday problems. You will learn about consequences of all behaviors, good and bad. Making responsible grown-up decisions. Doing the right thing for others in your life. Thinking about others before yourself when making choices and holding yourself and others accountable for all actions.

Other parents will probably have some very good insight and experiences you can learn from. They may even have some suggestions that you haven't even thought of. Most importantly

you will see you are not alone.

9

ATTEND EVERY THERAPY SESSION

Therapy. It's the time to face your issues head on. More than likely your social worker has mandated therapy. It's recommended you not only attend, but work on yourself. This is the perfect opportunity to do that while your kids are away. For once it's all about you.

Therapy can be painful. Breaking your arm can be less painful than digging up a painful past. If you can endure the pain, you might like what you find and find what you need. Hopefully, you can find a good therapist who can help ease you through the rocky road you are likely to travel. Therapy can be one of the most important things you will do for yourself. I would like to encourage you to be open with your therapist and above all, be honest. You can get the most support from your therapist with an open and honest relationship.

Whether you are truly interested in improving your situation or trying to appease your social worker, make sure you attend your scheduled appointments. Most therapists have policies in place that state if you are late for an appointment, you must reschedule. Those late/missed appointments will be noted and sent to your social worker. Again arrive early and ready to roll. If an emergency should arise and you will be late or need to reschedule, call your therapist so you don't have a "no show" on your record.

PART TWO

At this point you're probably starting to see every decision you make will be up for judgment. With that in mind this is a good time to look at those habits that might not be acceptable. Again, if the things you do are a secret, it's probably going to hamper having your kids at home.

Even while your kids are living in another home, your lifestyle will come under scrutiny. I understand that everything isn't everyone's business, but I will say this numerous times-you are under a microscope. The way your house looks, the money you spend, the people you choose to hang out with might be up for discussion. Also, the money you earn and how you earn it. How will you provide for your children? Can you feed them? What will you feed them? Do you have pets and can you care for them?

Truth is everyone's lives are up for some sort of scrutiny. Not everyone gets in trouble for their decisions and not everyone gets caught making bad choices. Some people seem to fly under the radar. We can't speak for others and how they manage their lives, but you can manage yours and live proud for yourself and your family.

10

CLEANLINESS IS NEXT TO GODLINESS

There's one thing you can't hide. A dirty house. The level of filth may come into question. Cleanliness is a value and it may not be one of your family values to live in a clean home. Some people cringe at the sight of a little dirt on the floor and take their shoes off before entering the house. You may not be one of those people and that's alright.

Some things to consider. Can you easily move about the home? Can you sit on the couch? Can you sit at the kitchen table to eat? Are there clean dishes? Is there food in the house? Are the animals trained to go outside? Can you sleep in the beds? Do the beds have sheets? Are the sheets clean? What about the towels and clothes? Are there garage items in the house, such as gasoline or oil?

While some may argue these aren't reasons for your kids to live with foster families, I assure you a Social Worker will disagree. You may take every class required, get off drugs, stop drinking but if you can't do simple everyday things, you might hit a road block.

Now don't get discouraged if you haven't been taught to clean or the job is too big and overwhelming. Start with the basics. Clean off the couch and the kitchen table. Don't be afraid to throw things away. Find a box and pick up all clothes on the floor. Decide what to keep and what to throw away. If any animals have urinated or worse on any items of clothing or blankets, it might be wise to throw them out. If you don't have enough clothes to throw things away and cannot afford to buy new, wash everything with soap and bleach, fold and put in a dresser or hang in the closet. Again, these are basic everyday things, and you will be expected to maintain your home.

Beds will need clean sheets. Please don't allow your kids or yourself to sleep on mattresses that aren't covered. Sheets should be washed about once a week unless someone wets the bed, then they should be washed immediately. For some, these are basics, but for others they are new skills to be learned. Keeping up every day may be the next challenge. I met a mom whose daughter wet the bed fairly regularly. To teach her daughter a lesson, she didn't always change the sheets after she wet the bed.

Dedicate a few minutes every night before you go to bed to wash the dishes, put dirty clothes in a hamper and clear off the table and couch. It's a step. Maybe not a huge one, but it will make a big difference.

LORI HAMILTON

11

MONEY

The manner in which money comes to you and where it goes

may also be addressed. Do you have a job? Can you cover your

bills with it? Making sure there is electric, heat and water are

essential. I knew a family who lost their heat in the spring because

they couldn't pay the bill, but they assumed since there was firewood and a fireplace it was fine. It wasn't. Ultimately, the kids were removed for neglect.

Utilities are basics. Internet, cell phones and cable are not. You don't need the Internet. You can go to the library for the Internet. If you can't pay the water, gas and electric bills, please don't get internet. Internet is usually required for school aged-children to do their homework or for job hunting. Most companies have online applications and won't even talk to you if you walk in the door. Go to the library. The kids can usually use school computers. Not having the internet is a huge inconvenience, but you need utilities. As long as you don't have utilities, your kids won't be returned.

Cell phones are another issue. They are important, however you can have a land line. Land lines are usually cheaper than cell phones. Cell phones are important in so many ways and there are ways to get one cheap, but there needs to be a phone at home. It is recommended that all children home alone are able to call 911. There shouldn't be people in a house where there is no access to emergency services. A note about cell phones. Most people know about prepaid phones. They are a really good option, and for 30 to 50 dollars, you can get a month of unlimited everything.

12

WORK

For most working is a fact of life. All your mandates can make

it hard to keep employment. Employers may not care about your

troubles, and might not be so willing to let you off work to attend the numerous classes that are required. Unfortunately you may have to come clean with your boss about your personal business. If your boundaries have remained intact, your employer may not know what's going on at home.

I knew a young man who was in a management position in his job. He gave up that position and took a pay cut to be able to make all of his mandates. Fortunately, his boss allowed that. All of his days off were used for visits and classes. He ended up taking another job part-time to help cover expenses. He was exhausted, but after his kids came back, he was able to scale back his schedule. His boss even gave him back his management position because he showed up every day, and gave one hundred percent to his work.

If you are lucky, you will find classes that work around your schedule and you can keep your job. Living in a city is usually a bonus as there are more options. However, you may have to consider a different job if there is interference. Of course keeping your routine is best, but it is not always possible.

Truthfully, it's a bit of a catch 22. On one hand you are expected to keep a job to show you can care for your kids, but you're also expected to attend classes, visits, court dates, etc. The more likely you are to pull it all off, the better your chances of reunification.

LORI HAMILTON

13

PETS

I'm inclined to say no pets! If caring for children was difficult,

then caring for pets will be no different. Pets require attention,

food, water, love and shelter. If your dog is tied to a tree outside

your house, find a new home for your pet immediately. If someone

turned you in for improper care of a child, those same people will turn you in for improper care of a pet. Often, the two go hand in hand. Pets need care just as children do. There is no reason to get one when your life is unstable. It's a tough situation if you've had a pet for years. Maybe you've had a dog that has grown up with the kids. That is really a tough decision to make. You might need to ask yourself some tough questions.

1. Have you always properly cared for this pet?

2. When was the last time this pet has been to the vet?

3. Is there always adequate pet food in the house?

4. Are you able to give the pet the time and love it requires?

5. If you answered yes to all of the above, ask yourself what went wrong while caring for you children?

I went to a home once where the placement of the children was in jeopardy. The family had two kittens. The kids loved the kittens, however the parents never had cat food. The kittens were skinny and hungry. The kittens would eat anything, and therefore the family fed them anything. Needless to say, the kittens were removed, and so were the kids. The charge against the parents was "general neglect." The same applied to the kittens. The parents truly did not think they had neglected the kittens because they fed them. Since they never fed them cat food, the food they were given was not right for the kittens and the kittens lacked proper nutrition and were starving. Think of this, if you only eat cat food instead of human food, you will lack everything you need to live and you will starve.

No dogs, no cats, no rabbits, no guinea pigs, no rats, no snakes, no spiders, no ant farms, no fish, no hermit crabs, no pet rocks. No pets! This rule should apply as long as there is an open CPS case, unless you are 100% certain you are giving them everything they need to thrive.

14

FOOD AND NUTRITION

Children who do not eat a proper diet can suffer from lack of brain development and malnutrition. Without proper brain development, a child cannot learn. One crucial element a social worker will look at when making recommendations to reunify your family, is whether or not there is an adequate amount of food in the house. In addition to having food in the house, that food must be fit for consumption. Is your food supply fresh or expired? Sometimes people will shop, forget what they bought and it will sit and expire. It happens, however this might be a good time to take a good look. All boxed and canned food need to be looked at. Canned food is packed for longevity, but after 12 months its usually time to toss it. Check expiration dates and throw things out by those dates.

Children need ample protein, grain, vegetables and fruit. Young children should drink whole milk. Picky eaters are especially hard to feed, but children need these things in their diet. Most children don't love broccoli, but it can be disguised. Cut it up into small pieces and mix it in with other foods. Kids will do whatever possible to get out of eating what they don't like. If one of the issues you are facing is a child with nutrition issues, you will need to work extra hard.

I knew a mom who said her son wouldn't eat. She said "I can't just sit and watch him eat, I don't know what to do?" Actually, since malnutrition was an issue for this family, she did need to sit and watch him eat. We suggested she have family meal time, so she could monitor his eating habits and model good eating habits for him. It turns out every time the family ate together, the child would eat his meal too. Maybe he was lonely, at meal time.

Let's look at the food groups. Protein is critical to a child's growth and development. It's essential for bones, skin, muscles and the immune system. Good sources of protein are milk, soy milk, beef, chicken pork, egg yolk, beans, cheese, yogurt, cottage cheese, turkey, fish, nuts, peanut butter, beans, and tofu. Make sure protein of some sort is given to your child at every meal.

Grains are carbohydrates that will give your child energy. Children should eat whole grains every day. Oats, whole wheat breads and pasta are full of fiber and B vitamins, vitamin E, magnesium, potassium, selenium and iron which are important to a growing body.

Vegetables and fruit need be plentiful. 1 ½ cups for kids 4 to 8 years old and 2 ½ cups for kids 9 to 13. Seem like a lot? It is. Kids and adults need dark leafy greens and colorful fruits and vegetables. A good rule is the darker and more colorful, the better the chance for adequate nutrients. You may have to hide them in various other foods. You can hide vegetables in almost anything. You can mix them in any meat, potatoes, rice, sandwiches, and pasta. Use your imagination. Choosemyplate.gov is an excellent resource.

15

CARING FOR YOURSELF

I would like to suggest that you spend some time taking care of yourself. You will be much better equipped to care for others if you can care for yourself first. Maybe make a list of things that you enjoy. Things you liked before you were a parent. Exclude illegal things and start practicing healthy living. Your self-confidence will likely go up if you are feeling healthy. Implementing some healthy eating habits and exercise is a gift you can give yourself and your family.

You may feel like you're not allowed to be happy. Truth is you will be a far more qualified parent if you can show your kids love, happiness and laughter. Your kids are more likely to be happy if you are. It's a win, win. What are some things you've enjoyed in the past? Maybe spend some time thinking this through. Make a list.

If there are some demons you're struggling with, please find healthy ways to fight them. Forgiveness is huge and carrying around guilt and anger is a poison. Yes, you have a right to your feelings and maybe you're not ready to forgive others, but forgiving yourself can be quite freeing. A good therapist can help with this.

Another good practice during this time is creating routines. Set up schedules for yourself. Kids thrive with schedules. It may not be something you've ever done, in fact it may feel a little rigid if you're not used to it. Try going to bed at the same time every night and getting up at the same time every day. Kids are easier to manage when they are rested and parents are better parents when they are rested.

Prayer, meditation or some sort of spiritual practice can bring peace and calm to a chaotic situation. Finding peace isn't about religion, it's about an internal calm that allows you to wake up every day and handle whatever life throws at you. Truth is hard times happen to everyone at some point, being prepared emotionally will likely help the outcome. Freaking out is NEVER going to improve a crisis situation.

16

REVIEW

Review, Review, Review. Always be reviewing your mandates to make sure nothing has slipped passed you. You may be tackling several mandates at once and realize you never paid your restitution, or you forgot to get a drug test. Again, if you forget something you will be looked upon as someone who doesn't care.

Don't let this happen, your actions will be pivotal. Your understanding of your actions will make or break the end result of your case.

Review your parenting homework. Review what was taught in class. Review all notes you made and whatever other parents have suggested. Spend time thinking about what your instructor and other parents are saying. Everyone's style of parenting is different and they will all bring something useful to the table.

Find an understanding of why drinking and drugs aren't working in your life. Spend time in honest review on the role drugs have played in your life. Be completely honest with yourself. If there has been even one time when it has interfered with your ability to parent, that one is too many times.

Look around your home; Is it clean? Can you sit on the couch? Are the dishes clean and in the cupboard? Is the kitchen floor clean or do your socks stick when you walk? Are there animal feces on the floor? When was the last time the sheets were washed and the beds made? Take time to look at your environment.

What are you working on in therapy? Do you like who you are or is there room for improvement? Most people have room for improvement. Make a list of all the things you can improve on. Start with your environment, the people who you spend time with and the places you choose to go. Your daily habits and routines are important too. Write it down and decide how you feel about your life. It's your life, make it a life you and your family can be proud of.

Every day is a new day to start over. Please try and find forgiveness for yesterday and embrace today as a new start to whatever you want for you and your family.

Sources:

http://www.acf.hhs.gov/sites/default/files/cb/afcarsreport22.pdf

http://www.acf.hhs.gov/sites/default/files/cb/afcarsreport20.pdf

http://www.liftingtheveil.org/foster14.htm

Department of Health and Human Services

National Child Abuse Coalition

http://www.nationalchildabusecoalition.org/

Preliminary FY1, 2012 Estimates as of November 2013. No. 20

United States Department of Agriculture, 2014.

Choosemyplate.gov

Childhelp.org

ABOUT THE AUTHOR

Lori was a single mom to three daughters and worked for 5 years supporting families in Wraparound and Success First. Lori has learned so much working with families who found themselves with kids who were either in placement or on their way to a placement. Lori is earning her degree in psychology and lives in the mountains with her husband Greg and dogs Ty and Stella

ABOUT THE ILLUSTRATOR

Taylor currently works as a graphic designer for an upscale flooring company in San Diego after earning her degree in graphic design. She lives in San Diego with her boyfriend Bradley.